CROSSING PLEASURE AVENUE

CROSSING
PLEASURE AVENUE

POEMS

KAREN HILDEBRAND

© 2018 Karen Hildebrand
Cover photograph: Julio Cesar Martinez
Author Photo: Matthew Murphy
Cover and book design: adam b. bohannon
Book editor: Nicholas Oliver Moore
Published by Indolent Books,
an imprint of Indolent Art Foundation, Inc.
www.indolentbooks.com
Brooklyn, New York
ISBN: 978-1-945023-13-2

CONTENTS

PART I
Binomial Nomenclature 3
A History of Feminism 4
When We Lived on Pineview Lane 6
Sleep Apnea 7
The Haven 8
Dear John 9
We Need to Talk 10
A Walk Down the Aisle 11

PART II
The Great Milky Way 14
Learner's Permit 16
First Day of Spring, Giddy and Swollen 17
All-American Activities 18
Tough Bird 19
The Sixties, Explained 20
Softball Game at the Church Picnic 21
Seasonal Affect Disorder 22
Sum Total 24

PART III
Three Hour Train Delay 28
Home, ca 1951 29
Good Fortune 30
Talking About the Heat 32
Learning to Paddle a Canoe 33
Emily Dickinson's Fruitcake 34
All In 35
Dia de los Muertos 36

Earthquake Weather   37
Standing in Line to Register for the Moon   38

PART IV

Year of the Monkey   40
Women Like Us   41
A Woman in the Sun   42
The Year of No Men   43
After the Wine-Tasting   44
Femme Fatale   45
Test Drive With Einstein   46
Winter   47
Too Late   48
B Movie Fashion on the Red Carpet   49
This is the Revolution   50

PART V

Spiritual Practices of Bears   52
Blossoming   53
Biography of a Sunflower   54
Sewing Lessons   55
Drought   56
Flood   57
Ode to My Bunion   58

PART VI

Sugar Suite   60

Part VII

At Farley's   72
Happy Birthday, Libra   74
The Night Chuck Prophet Played Slim's   76
Googling My Ex   77
Crash (San Francisco, 1999)   78

Cleaning the Closet   81
Evidence   83
Two Figures in a Landscape   84
The Day the Widows Hijack the C Train   85
Four a.m.   86
Crossing Pleasure Avenue   87
On Leaving   89

Acknowledgements   91
About the author   95
About Indolent Books   95

PART I

Binomial Nomenclature

I was raised by insects
who left me with spinal
abnormalities and an appetite
for silk. As a species, we tend
to be very private, hiding
our delicate exoskeletons under hats
that do little to flatter. Recently,
I was visited by a clan of centipedes,
who refer to each other with affection
and nicknames one needs a chart
to track. I am enthralled with ants.
Sensing sugar from fifteen floors down,
they chain smoke until every last one
has breached the windowsill.
As a child, I would study the family tree
in my grandmother's bible, tracing
my finger backward among the branches.
There is no evidence I was switched
at birth. Back then, I had no reason
to doubt the space beneath my name
would one day be filled with anything
less than desire.

A History of Feminism

I. Cowboys and Indians
The neighbor boys Kenny and Jimmy tied
me to the fence in our backyard lean-to
fort and I liked it. I was a smoke plume,
a cat's eye plucked. I was every girl
embroidering pillowcases while perched
on a hope chest. I had no compass for my
notions, no envy for my noble brother,
his Stetson or the stallion he galloped
in his dreams. I saw magic straddling
the loins of an Argentine tango.

II. She Thinks She's Brenda Starr
Aging sex symbol in red leggings
and ruffles. It's a shame she hasn't "reframed,"
like the rest of us, a band of post-posts
who weren't rock stars. We spent our juicy years
with laundry or typewriters, a little love
in the afternoon sometimes. Her platinum
curls still bounce. Consider all the trips
to Venus and back for those peachy cheeks,
the way she puckers her brow in thought.

III. Pussy
I once had a cat who charmed everyone
she met. I was not immune. She would plop
herself indecently on her back and expose
her tender belly for stroking, her green gaze
half-mast through her lashes could cloak you

with desire even as she drew her claws
when you came too close. *Look don't touch.*

IV. Bucket List
Me? I just want to be kissed. As in excavation,
the kind that will leave you sniffling, your pores
gasping even as you raise your chin for more.
I want to be kissed like I was fine bone china
watch where you put your hands, and only once.
I want to press lips so hard the bruise becomes
sentient, *my what a strong gaze you have*, boring
deep with one thought: survive.

When We Lived on Pineview Lane

I. Deep into sap and damp, their boots sink into gravel like cookie-cutters. A fox crosses their path at dusk, the final hill, when he starts an argument to distract her from the effort to climb.

II. She feels like the eight-point buck, she says, blinded in the headlights. Or maybe she's the slick dark road. He sits behind the wheel, speechless, seatbelt buckled, head bowed, shattered windshield glass in his lap.

III. From the kitchen window she watches a bear rip apart the compost bin, cedar-staked and substantial, tossing aside a slab so heavy the two of them, with effort, cannot replace it.

Sleep Apnea

That's me behind the wheel, head thrust forward, over the limit in my 280Z, in a rush to Lake City. That's him, drunk, down at the Oak Room, Budweiser lifted in his hand then dropped like an ax. Together, we are a window shade unsprung, mattress ticking pressed into the side of a face.

Next thing I know, we're two martinis sleepwalking, taking Polk and Geary at a tilt, groping at fog. That must be some other woman in copper taffeta polka dots, pursed lips, missing the punchline.

Then came the year of loss: the cat, the ovaries, the him. He stood me up for—"Marshmallows? How did you know?"—the Jungian symbol for *fuck you*.

There's just not that much good sex left in the world. Hell, when it's dark at four, who can say what's normal? Please wake me. Every now and then, I forget to breathe.

The Haven

A club, hidden in a forgotten strip mall
outside Baltimore. Guys out front hawk
bags full of bootleg. Inside, Michael on horn,

Zack on sax. A man takes a seat down front,
nods to the stogies at the bar, smoking
the tunes. *No beer on tap tonight, man,*

no Cuervo. No matter. What is, will be
just fine. In walks a woman in leopard capris,
platform shoes teetering past the edge.

The man leans back, closes his eyes, lets
the groove smooth his engraved face. She
pauses at his booth, hand on her hip.

His bass line feels her melody—Saturday
night, a wink of a moon. He opens one eye,
pats the empty space and she sits down.

Dear John

Here's to your creamy neck, cold indifference,
the damp swipe of your tongue. I've cradled
you long into the night despite the constant flap
of your jaw. American Standard, Kohler, Rohl.
I've loved you all. I prefer you strong
and silent—the way you were in Germany,
all that ergonomic restraint. You were
a little too earthy in Italy. Sorry.
In France, I couldn't comprehend
what you wanted. I am fluent
in flush, and the click click
clicking of high heels in perpetual
retreat. Please. don't. hurt. me.

We Need to Talk

Just look at him
leaning forward, straddling
the chair, legs looped
around the rungs, ballcap
bill smudged from his
earnest tugs, picking
at the paint beneath his nails,
facing the constant jiggle
of my foot. A fly lights
on the table between us.
I strangle every drop
from my teabag.

A Walk Down the Aisle

They said it would take a century
to get from I do to we're done.

We'd have plenty of time
to uncake the mud from our shoes.

The photos reveal guests turning
to bow as we stand at the altar,

two cigarettes, lit
with what we called love.

PART II

The Great Milky Way

I have many reports
on the miseries of the milkman,

daughter of dairy folk that I am.
But the cows! The cows are lovely!

Holstein, Guernsey,
Belarus Red. Uncle Vern

used to hook them up
to machines that pulsed

the barn like a disco. Milk!
My happy place! Butter

churned from the froth!
Takes well to chocolate

and mama's boys.
It's the sweet bond of suckle

we wish we could return to.
In a bowl the Cheerios

always run out first.
Snow White, a shapely vixen,

bottled with a pleated cap,
wholesome as Nancy Drew.

"Farming is hard," said Uncle Vern
before he died. "Damn you,

Vern," said his wife, after.
When he was sad, he ate

Wonder Bread soaked in milk
from a glass with a spoon.

Learner's Permit

Like marshmallows bobbing
in Kool-Aid, we are three
high-school girls in my mother's
green Corvair, fragrant
with Wrigley's and wet wool,
blue streetlamp glow, sliding
sideways down an icy hill
to the snowy ditch, a streak
of red brake lights ahead,
gear shift knob buzzing
in my hand. Like falling
in love underwater, a bell
going off, yellow flash,
my mother's fuschia
pajamas peeking from
the hem of her winter coat.

First Day of Spring, Giddy and Swollen

I keep coming back to this photo of my dad's aunties:
five rifle toting, moonshine jugging ranch wives
lined up in sepia relief, circa 1930.
They're mugging, stealing a frame from a chicken scratch
life, homely and wrung out, their dresses stained
by the volcanos of their armpits, boots caked with dung
and spit, telling us, *Women are the bacon of this life*!

All-American Activities

I'm hanging off the cement lip
of the pool, eavesdropping
on Mom and her cocktail onion
friends bobbing in the deep end.
"He calls her 'the housekeeper.'"
"I heard it was the brother, not the father."
"So awful, so young."
Next thing I know, I've lost my grip,
gone under, the sparkling voices
lost to a roaring in my head
that sounds like Lloyd Bridges
sucking air in his "Sea Hunt" scuba
gear. There was always a bad guy
with a knife, struggling to cut
the air hose. You knew it was over
when you saw the bubbles rising
and I wriggle like I'm fighting
for my life to grab the nearest jellyfish
thigh and grope my way back, spewing
indignation—I could have drowned!
My mother laughs and pulls me to her,
cigarette clenched between her teeth.
"There now, that wasn't so bad," she says,
turning back to breaking news.

Tough Bird

I've begun to smell
like my grandmother.
Not the one who wore lilacs
pinned to her pink Easter
boucle, white gloves,
Book of Common Prayer
ringed in gold. No,
I mean the other one
with large appetites—
Jim Beam, "shut-up and
deal me some decent cards,
goddammit," while tapping
ash from a Salem Menthol.
You could see the bacon grease
running down her living room
wall behind my grandfather,
chugging oxygen in his
scabby recliner.

Dim afternoons, spinning
on a ruby bar stool,
L&M Steakhouse, where
we all gathered when
I was a kid—my uncles, Dad,
Aunt Phyllis, their cackling
laughter, large-nosed barbs.
Where are they now
that I've begun to smell
like a woman who can hold her own?

The Sixties, Explained

Leave it to Beaver
It was that slime bag Eddie Haskell who outed Beaver the day he showed up at school in a dress. The Beev just doesn't get it. Ward loads his pipe and sinks into his newspaper. June starts another batch of chocolate chip cookies. "Shucks," says Wally. "Raising me must have been a cinch."

Gilligan's Island
The professor has cultivated a variety of cannabis that smells like burgers sizzling on the grill. When it comes to exit strategies, Gilligan and The Skipper can talk themselves silly.

Mister Ed
The neighbors are amused by the talking horse bit, but if Wilbur's wife has her way, the man will soon be on Thorazine.

That Girl!
Donald brings home takeout every night for a reason. When Marlo Thomas opens her refrigerator, she feels the rough velvet of church pew cushions on the backs of her thighs. The vegetable crisper is full of copper peonies and jelly drips through the shelf rungs like red rain. At the height of passion, she calls out the name, Casper.

The Andy Griffith Show
Opie is not the happy go lucky kid he once was, not that anyone in Mayberry would notice. Aunt Bee is buzzed on Adderall. Barney Fife is wrapped up in a Dungeons & Dragons marathon and hasn't left his basement in days. Andy thinks a walk down to the fishing hole is the answer to pretty much everything.

Softball Game at the Church Picnic

A speeding ball could
ping apart this wishbone.
A hit to the solar plexus,
lungs like lilies, waxy
mouth gaspless, useless
mitt still on my hand.
Moms on the sidelines, dads
at the smoky grill, sorry
guy at bat, all stop
to watch a bubble of air
raise its skinny arm.

Seasonal Affect Disorder

Summer
When some move to country
homes, I move to my sofa
to lie under a lazy cross breeze
that whispers of childhood, the tang
of grass and dried sweat, a hot night
running with my brother and a pack
of kids until our dad whistles.

Fall
*There are no female Ginkgo trees
in Manhattan*, says a gardener friend
as we stroll down Lafayette in Brooklyn,
the reek of vomit rising from underfoot.
Ginkgo fruit as it decomposes, he tells me.
Call it the stink of fully consummated love.

Winter
I sink into night, hot as a feverish child,
who might have been me, toddling
to my mother as she slept soundly
next to dad, asking to press my back
to the fetal cave of her body until I felt safe
and she walked me back to my room,
preparing me well to sleep alone.

Spring
It never smells like vomit in Manhattan
where the male Ginkgo thrives alone,

*unless someone is actually sick,
my friend goes on to say. In the
unfulfilled quest for love, the males
release more spore. This pollen
makes many of us miserable.*

Sum Total

I was conceived in the house of 2211 (Center Street).
These are power numbers
An auspicious sign, multiplied—two two one one
the world proceeding in pairs.
I flipped my luck and lived at one one two two (Gaylord)
with a gay lord, no less.
When is 2 a binary number and when is it a duel?
We added up the columns and split.

Single or double? This is always the question
for those born under a Gemini moon.
Lesson #2,119 (South Sherman).
I took back my family name and lived
under the sign of restless:
3895 Rings of Saturn
2222 House of Chaos
Venus rising
Room of Sorrow
Jellyfish Cocoon.

My sun is in the number 6—
the great explorer,
6 digit salary
Sex, serpentine
fetal, the frame
for all smart quotations
106 (Pineview)
616 (Carolina)
61 (West 10th)
Where is my six now?

I'm back to simple math.
Two aught one (Clinton)
solve for double vision
minus the repetition
wobbly, bobbly, no love for me.
If it's all a numbers game
dear wheel of fortune
why not throw me a lucky 7?
All sharp edges, slanty sideways glances
a crushed velvet fainting couch.

PART III

Three Hour Train Delay

Dusk lies across the Hudson like a bride's veil,
silky water a rippling muscle of the groom's arm
she holds with one hand, the train of her dress
could be the river itself flowing outside
the grimy railcar window where I wait
on the opposite shore, a gown swirls
at the ankles of a solitary lighthouse.
Everywhere I look, there is dancing.

Home, ca 1951

I was but a glimmer in the backseat
of that jalopy, the year Kerouac ended
his opus—all the jitter and yakety,
wind flapping his hound dog tongue.
Jack made it look easy, all that malarkey.
I'm the stuff that made his eyelid twitch:
What about the mortgage? What about
Blue Cross Blue Shield on the road?
It's no fun to be no fun. I'm the bologna
sandwich his girl insisted he pack,
It's a long way to Toledo. I'm the way
he cried a little when he asked
if she'd be true. I'm the relief she felt
when the screen door banged shut. I'm
miller moths doing the chachacha
in the porchlight. I'm dinner dishes
settling into the suds with a sigh.

Good Fortune

If you wear the dress of another woman, it means you will sleep with her lover.

If you look forever at a face that is dear to you, you will disappear.

If you climb Mt. Olympus, the hair on your arms will beg for lightning.

While trying to bleed a turnip, you will breed a colony of black flies to kiss your lipstick.

If your idea of traveling light is a square dance, you will turn and turn and turn.

If you fancy yourself a new age Odysseus, then Circe will stall you with vodka martinis and a gift of shoes to bind your feet.

You will see the dreams of a stranger when you close your eyes, the way a cat adjusts to blindness.

May you bathe in rose petals and the juice of a dozen organic lemons. The fortune teller will be angry you wasted her time.

Later, she will demand you return it.

Facing backward on the train is not the same as hindsight.

If you forget why you left home, your spine will begin to pull to the east to fill the absence of the west, and there will be birch trees
wading in the snow.

Talking About the Heat

Summer is for sale—two
bunches for ten dollars
at the corner bodega.
Taxis on Sixth Avenue
are a field of marigolds.
The a/c thrums and stalls
like an infestation of cicadas.
Dusk rinses its stale mouth
in the Hudson and a rat
collapses to fit a crack
in the black stallion night.
A miracle of fireflies
in Union Square, a mounted
cop releases the reins,
letting his steed go nose
to nose with a wriggling
Jack Russell terrier.

Learning to Paddle a Canoe

I get that it's a simple matter of physics.
For every action, there is an equal
and opposite reaction, like love.
I can't tell a fulcrum from a fish.
When I dip an oar into the surface,
my face ripples. So, this is joy!
The lower hand serves as a pivot
to the lever action. It's somewhat easier
than I imagined, to navigate these waters.
Once the stroke is completed, relax.
Endurance will come naturally
with practice. I raise my paddle
and drift near a pair of loons.

Emily Dickinson's Fruitcake

Butternut squash and kale stew, eaten
as the British do, while wearing paper
crowns. This is how we spend Christmas,
two women old enough to no longer
be charmed by Santa. We toast to the health
of our online-dating personae and leave
the warmth of the hearth to join our fellow
heathen at the foot of Saks Fifth Avenue.
I like the fish tank window, filled with shiny
trombones, blue notes floating at the hips
of a sea nymph. All around us, street peddlers
hawk fake Chanel as we elbow our way
to the cradle of Baby Jesus. I consider
the bit of fruitcake tucked in my bag for later—
crusty brown sugar molasses, currants, nuts.
"This is Emily Dickinson's recipe,"
my friend had said. Emily, who wisely
never left her house. Sirens woke me
early today in cold-brew Brooklyn, so far
from stables and hay. What is it about
a six-story-tall Norwegian Spruce?

All In

Some say a sneeze is a small
death. I prefer premonition. We say
"bless you" to ward off evil, as if
disaster can escape through the nose,

an involuntary snort of insect wing
or ash, that flutters in the common air
our lungs share, twenty times per minute,
with each of us in this crowded room.

Look around. That fellow on the C train
stutters a sermon that if you let
your mind go, comes through
clean as cotton: Consider this a song.

Consider the cup you don't want to share.
Its liquid will flow through me into you
through pipes, gullies, the rivers
of our unstoppable dreams.

Consider the force that guides
the muddy tracks of your ambition
down the stairs of morning, the way
you brush your teeth at night,

but skip the floss, the way
snowflakes drag the clouds
to the ground and allow us
to grind them under our boots.

Dia de los Muertos

We take our pallor from a tube,
white face to hollow the eyes
and paint our rosy lips with bony teeth.

The crowd forms on Mission—
Mayan dancers shake
their bells and beaded sticks.

We are calling in the souls
with sugar skulls, incense,
salt, and song.

But how will you find me?
A musky trail of marigolds?
A pack of smokes, more likely—

I saved your last in a Ziploc.
Tonight, my altar glows. The purple
sequins of my skirt could spiral

from here to Venus. The souls approach
like fire ants. I am calling, you are
crawling farther from me every year.

Earthquake Weather

When the sky clears, we all go
to North Beach. We leave
the frowning barrista alone

with her tattooed fists,
shake the dust from our
pillbox hats of lavender straw,

soft with age, crumpled rose.
On a day like this, our lips
bloom. Electricity in the air

raises the hair on our arms
as if we are standing at timberline,
too close to God. Not even

the camera can sit still on a day
like this. Edges fuzz, lines go
jiggy. Let the gown slide

from your shoulder, savor
the delirious crackle and coil.

Standing in Line to Register for the Moon

We've come straight from yoga on an icy path, wary
of taking the fall that could land us squarely into old age.

Once inside we fuss with the hat, the mittens, the gummy
wad of tissue that must be shifted from hands to armpits

to pockets in order to slide change into our wallets. Puddles
form at our feet and a stringy kid wields a mop. We stumble

in the dark while thinking we should have asked for
the senior discount, after all. But really, how can an extra

two dollars possibly matter on the moon? The rustling
of down jackets is as annoying as the return of cicadas

after seventeen silent years, then dies off when George Clooney
rises three stories tall on the screen—clear green eyes, big

teeth, creatively tousled hair. No one seems alarmed when we
exit into startling light, where a yellow school bus idles.

Am I the only one who remembers that handsome devotee
of Reverend Sun Young Moon? He invited me to a summer

cookout, then tricked us all onto a bus to god knows where.
Have I learned nothing? I think, as I hold out my hand

like a school girl at a dance, eager to say *yes*.

PART IV

Year of the Monkey

It started with Bowie and Rickman—
the internet went nutz over that.
Then Hicks, Haggard and Prince,
like some aging rockstar law firm.
Along with my ovaries, I've lost
the ability to weep. Today's weather
is online shopping in record amounts.
I have enough backdated email from you
to collapse a crane, and this pair
of useless waterproof shoes.

Women Like Us

fall madly in love
with companion animals
and vintage dresses
that reek of other women.
We listen like geisha
skilled in the art of tea
but ask us for help,
we won't return
your call. Women
like us nibble all day
on a racy bit, then gasp
when it goes straight
to our hips. We don't
know what we want,
yet always reject
your advice. We're
perfectly logical—
like a bobsled steered
by a snake. Even Brando
would flinch, caught
in our glare. Women
like us want to become
the men we think
we love. We're guileless
as you could want.

A Woman in the Sun

A painting by Edward Hopper

Standing naked in her room
against the glare of his angular light,
she doesn't know we're watching.
Feels the breeze riffing the corner
curtain billowing her single bed,
messy fleshy fish of her thigh
biting. *Yes, my darling,*
as she brings the bony cigarette
to her mouth, the breath out
and the next one, stale
mourning breath.
I've missed you
not, I'll miss you.
She has removed him
like a dress that binds at the waist
kicked under the bed with the toppled night.

The Year of No Men

It was the year we discovered compostable flatware. We carried eco-friendly utensils in our pockets. We were particularly fond of sporks. They came in handy during meetings when we needed to stab our own hands to keep from saying yes.

That was the year we became no-men.

Estrogen reigned. So much so, the market became saturated. We exceeded capacities of our bras and shoelaces. The frequency of hysterectomies grew sharply in an attempt to manipulate demand.

We looked forward to menopause to get some relief. We no longer wore cotton or ate strawberries. We braided our hair with obsolete shopping lists.

One night Whole Foods ran out of kale. A quiet panic ensued and we understood this was the beginning of the collapse. We were greatly relieved the next day when it was all back.

After the Wine-Tasting

Despite the joke that only a poet
would turn a bouquet of violets
into violence, I'm behind the wheel,
driving a country road late at night,
when the car dies, lights go, radio slurs
like those alien spaceship encounters
where they suck up all the power
and then the moon explodes.
We watch through the windshield,
but the moon is really the sun,
which, of course, scares the bejesus out of me.
Kim and I look at each other—never mind,
she's been dead since 1999—and duck
into the back seat, our car gone off into the ditch.
Here comes chaos, roving bands, leather vested
scavengers, heads bandaged, dripping chains. This,
after a perfectly sedate evening, full-bodied red,
Chris's "soft and warm women," cheeses, figs.

Femme Fatale

We wash ashore with the incoming tide,
to lounge among the rocks. We dry
our seaweed locks, lamenting
how the years have robbed them
of their sheen.
Gossiping, harboring secrets,
we're at home here, blending
perfectly with the shale,
a hint of russet and aqua,
sun glinting off our scales.

A mermaid is a yoga pose, a myth.
Siren, sweetheart, bitch. A friend
who puts you down, then
calls you "sister." The mere sight of us
can be disaster. You can smell the kelp
on our breath, and sometimes
the slime is overwhelming.
The way we yammer on—
the new sailor doesn't cut it,
how we long to fall, fall, fall.

Test Drive With Einstein

I'm trying to sell him
my Volvo. He's hesitant.
There's a stutter
in the gear shift,
he says he's single,
married Anne Waldman
for about a minute.

Or maybe
that was a different
test drive—I swear
it was him. Same Volvo,
the strip of chrome
reattached with screws
to the front left fender.

Winter

Looks aren't everything, the way mothers are for baby seals,
the accordion player for the monkey.

Bonding is nothing but oxytocin. A little before dinner and off
you go into unprotected sex and apartment therapy.

In other words, look for cherry blossoms. When they're late,
it kills the mood.

Cozy and crazy are easily confused.

An old man waking from surgery with a tube down his throat.
His angry eyes. The woman beside him, doing the best she can.

If you flex your ankle a certain way as you head down to the
subway, you'll drop and slide like a dish into homebase.

What will happen when you have forgotten your best moves?
What will happen to the words coronary bypass, do not
    resuscitate?

There's no such thing as wait your turn.

A pair of watery eyes watching.

Too Late

I envy blueberries,
the way they are contented
with their state of round,
the dotted swiss they make
of muffins, the carton
where they snuggle up.
They feel no need
to be strawberries
or yearn for a pair
of Jimmy Choo's.
And when that dab of mold
turns up to end a short
but vivid life, straight
to the compost heap they go.

B Movie Fashion on the Red Carpet

Wasp Women, their eyes shrouded in purple satin,
translucent wings sprouting between their shoulders

Runaway Daughters in pastel capris, shirt tails tied
to frame their jailbait midriffs, next to *Hot Rodders
Who Make Speed their Creed*

We wonder aloud whether the *Men Are From
Mars*—certainly their big hats would suggest
they have a lot on their minds

My favorite is *Love-Hungry Monsters
from Hell*, their khaki shirts as ripped as their abs

It's one disaster after another

Three Zombie Teens, wearing beaded
off-the-shoulder gowns at ten in the morning

This is the Revolution

Last night at the open mic, it was rock
paper scissors. Cowboys. Conquistadors.
Artists, all of us, itching for a fight.
As the night wore on, the crowd grew lusty
with weapons, all manner smuggled in:
Pencils, peace signs, religion, a shunt.
If looks could kill, we were dressed
in a lowcut gown and a diamond
the size of Jerusalem. Then,
from the stage: "Shut up you faggot!"
and like a hot wind at sunset
the audience rose, hoisting
bar stools into the exalted air
above their heads. I turned
to the guy at my side, "Are we
the only ones here without guns?"
"Speak for yourself," he said,
as he scratched his balls.
"We have to crack the salty bone
of contention from the rib
housed in our own cage.
The ankle bone hates
the shinbone, the heart's pissed off
at the lung. It's a virus we spread
when it hurts too much inside.
This is how change begins. We itch."

PART V

Spiritual Practices of Bears

What does it mean when your howling
wakes you? You are safe, wrapped in bunting,
the same linen used for the dead
smells like summer, sheets snapping
the line, warm breezes, rover red rover
waving wild children right over. It's hard

to fry an egg sunny side when the skillet
is set to scramble. Crack goes the shell,
you can feel the membrane rip. It never
happens the way you think it will. Consider
that you've lived longer than your favorite
shade of red. Brown bears in the wild
stand guard when one of them is dying.

Do they chant or pray? Or simply ward off
vultures so the soul can settle? I see
they've moved in next door. Tired
of the daily lament, another failure
of medicine. Don't be the woman who lies
naked and suffering on her tile floor
considering her options too late. Leave
your door unlocked. Let the bears unburden you.

Blossoming

My task is to stand in the orchard
and prune the buds. Tiny
five-petaled bells, pink,
each made to grow a peach,
more than one tree can sustain.
Which to pinch? What to spare?
I leave behind a trail to shrivel
so that one day in late August
you may swallow the plump wet prize.

Biography of a Sunflower

Lanky and awkward,
late bloomer of the season.
In the Hudson Valley
there is a massive
field of nothing but.
It goes on for acres,
like a parade of willowy
baton twirlers tossing
and tilting their spiky
heads full of brazen
thoughts that can
sometimes prove
too much for a timid
spine. And what
of the morning, when
we come over the rise
to find them slaughtered—
some might say
harvested—but
whose story is this
to tell? Are we sorry
or celebrating,
when we bring out
the vases at the end
of summer?

Sewing Lesson

The question on your face
tells me you're unfamiliar
with the procedure.
Watch, as we set out
the tools for an early
detection, cut a sure
soft line. The shears
make a satisfying crunch
as we crimp, bite by bite.
We'll take our time,
lay a pattern, smooth
the surface, pin it down.
After, we will knot it
into a locket to bear
like a cross. The body
will betray again.
These threads
that glow like pearls
across your skin.

Drought

I am a mud flat caked.
The lake I once contained,
so low the corpses stink.
My tongue is stiff as a perfect
credit score. It's enough
to make my tear ducts pool.
You could say, I've made
my bed. Let me be clear—
when I tell you my dream
of horses, their haunches
twitching with a lovely sweat,
it's my vagina speaking.
This is all a warning.
My broken trust, divining
blue veins of my hands
rising like rivers.

Flood

Water, with its clarity, its quench,
its great slop on the sidewalk
to wash away the pee.
Tears to clear the eyes,
salt to stain the hours. Hope
is nothing more than a swollen
roll of paper towels bobbing
down Broadway after the hurricane.
My good intentions overflow
the water tower of the building
where I live, salvation steeps
ankle deep in the hallway, risk
of electrocution notwithstanding.

Ode to My Bunion

My big toe is pumped
on potassium. Faced
with the purgatory of foot
cramps that turn me into
an insomniac salamander,
I'll do anything.

I'm a jumpy junkie
jonesing for a good vibe,
holding out my palm
on the plaza: Please,
my big toe needs air,
everyone stand back.

I need a panama hat
for my big toe, that's
how much space,
I say, and the passersby
look the other way,
bunions being out

this season. Don't tell
that to my big fat toe
when in full passion
of a crooked jag, raging
against the pinch
boxing in its soul.

PART VI

Sugar Suite

1.
Just look at her, leaning against the bar—
her gingerbread skin, the saucy flirt
of her icing skirt painted on like an apron.
Her over-plucked brows are cold war
spies above her Raisenette eyes.
She refuses an invitation to dance,
with the tired excuse that her feet
are like biscuits—one splays,
the other punches. It's a miracle
that cookie can stand on her own.
Look at the way she holds out
her arms for a hug, as if the world
was not a hungry mouth, eager
to devour her in two easy bites.

2.
For our first date
he took me to
the senior shuffle.
Men without teeth
danced in blue
booties. I wore my
best hues of game-
for-anything and moved
my hooves to match
the weaving
and bobbing,
waiting to go low
for the body shot
I knew was coming.

3.
Last night, I was a snake
and you were a lizard.
Today my skin is blooming
like a shattered windshield.
I envy your coat of armor,
the way you always blend in.
Spare me your hot breath
and the tragedy of your tail—
you'll grow another.
No matter how often I shed,
the stains I was born with
bleed through—a passport,
every blister and slight,
stamped there, indelible.

4.
He places his lips
to her ear, lodges
a strand of hair behind.
Is he whispering
or kissing—nose to cheek,
lip to lobe, brushing
a finger along her jaw?
She has a chin like a witch.
He shines her like Christmas.
Like a cat, he laps her up
from the far side of the bowl.
She's absolutely delicious!
I wrote this down so
I would remember.

5.
A tractor trailer jackknifed and lost
control of its cargo—a giant boulder,
pinkly porous. It wobbled, at first
nearly righting itself, then flopped
to the ground like a flounder. Wait,
is it a rock or a fish? you might ask.
But this is a dream and the characters
are written in the language of hope.
The fish was left to lie like a rock,
and over the seasons, the earth
swallowed it whole, leaving only
a bare plane visible in the dirt.
When you come upon it, you see
a giant vulva. It's famous in these parts.

6.
My landlady says she painted
the walls these colors to remind her
of her wedding and the joy her lover
served like a plate of cupcakes.
She has a name for this yellow.
I call it mustard. I can hear water
running somewhere. I can hear the hum
that says I'm home. I practice saying
butterscotch when I walk through
this door. The other room is tangerine,
the seedless variety, genetically modified.
We're all genetically modified.
"Buttercup," she says. "Golden
as an egg yolk straight from the coop."

7.
My heart has gone stiff
as a cage. I can feel it
crumbling—the once
creamy confection,
cinnamon and ginger,
that could melt easy
as butter. You can't
say the word "heart"
in a poem. But you can
say "crumb cake" as in:
I left my crumb cake
out on the counter
and it shriveled into
a sack of worried ribs.

8.
The bald man is praying
for fire. He knows it will soon
be time to climb the stairs
to the attic. Every day at noon
the horn blasts and he remembers
how this siren was always
their song. There is no answer
to this riddle so don't ask me
why anyone would grow
a beard full of triangles.
I don't know what it means
to bow over burning branches.
I don't know what
is in the attic.

9.
It's like having box seats inside
the head of the Lilac Fairy, where
all are kind and mostly pastel.
The swords are sheathed, costumes
laid out—pearls and silk chiffon
in shades as sweet as hay.
She squeezes into her gown,
careful not to mash the raspberries,
flounces fat as creme fraiche.
The bodice holds her like a lover—
the one she loved the way a watermelon
wears its rind. The one she thinks of
first on waking, willing the loss
to *please, be a dream.*

10.
Dancing while seated
is like washing windows
while wearing a blindfold.
It starts with restless feet,
and ends with hip flexors
strapped tight as a trap.
When it comes to choosing
a partner, it's best to pad
the corners. Like clouds,
we must lie on our backs
and listen. The music
is a mourning dove at dawn,
everyone asleep, sun
kneeling on the creaky floor.

PART VII

At Farley's

William was the first to arrive. He washed his thermos in the sink behind the counter.

When Jon wanted to impress a woman, he brought up the Golden Mean. He threw back his head to laugh and you could see his coffee coated tongue.

Ralph said he could talk to a banana peel but he preferred women. He sipped espresso from a thimble between his thumb and middle finger.

Nick grew a beard on the right side of his face. He wore a straw fedora and it was always a late night at the Boom Boom Room, where he played blues piano but aspired to jazz.

"It's the way the Egyptians built the pyramids," Jon said. "The ratio of the longer side to the shorter."

It was all very silly, Karen thought, to consider romance at this juncture, as she wrote her poetry out by hand. Had a big callus from gripping her pen.

At nine sharp on Wednesdays the barista would shout, "Street cleaning!" and Jon would yell, "Fuck," grab his keys off the table and run.

Tom pulled out a Sharpie and drew a coffee cup on a page from the Bay Guardian and signed it so it would be worth a fortune after he died.

Curtis drew plans for a waste water system in a journal from the shelf and instructions for making a paper butcher's hat.

There was a spot in the floor that squished from dry rot. We were in love with the Ducati's lined up outside at the curb. Someone complained when Annie, the dog, stole a scone off a plate. The Health Department levied a fine.

Mostly we laughed. We thought we had time.

Jon returned, only to go on, "Of course, DaVinci was the master of pleasing proportion." No way he'd trust any gallery to represent him. That asshole Berggruen wouldn't pop for decent wine at his opening in 1993.

William screwed the lid on his thermos, folded the auto parts page into his pocket and drove off in the 1965 white Volvo he called Pearl.

Happy Birthday, Libra

here you are tender and tan
leading a march to the new year
with a confident stride in platform
stilettos your head full of candy
and aluminum you are the starch
in my petticoat you beautiful
dish of bone marrow and mouth
divide this blessing three ways
one for love one for freedom one
to strap to your wrist as you climb
the ladder to drape your kingdom
with blinking silver lights

and what do I bring to this
harvest of buttons and soup
I'm staring into a fisheye
fifth grade in my dad's pickup truck
broom bristles sticking up in back
a bantam rooster bouncing down
a dirt road lined by sycamores
to the lake to drop a line this is
my gift a still warm chocolate
cake not quite set in the middle
maple icing with walnuts between
dusty layers little pockets of song

the minute you walked through
the door I knew you were the one
for me forget the glycemic scale
it's the month of itching let's invite

our spirit animals to snuggle
we keep shedding and forgetting
it's a seasonal thing this dead
leaf on the sidewalk this fragrance
of patchouli and new lace-ups
I can feel myself drifting

in a way that will land me
face down on the lawn nibbling
an acorn with sharp little teeth
as if it could last the entire winter
crystalline morning shining
on the all-nighters the sugar-bingeing
the sunbathing the snap judgments
there is so much joy in the stunning light.

The Night Chuck Prophet Played Slim's

Her lover leaves her for a smoke,
alone on a bar stool, looped
on rock 'n roll. When she leans in
close to the guy at her side, speaks
into his ear to be heard over the band,
it looks to the lover like a kiss.
His glare darkens the mirror
she faces with a shrug, *A woman
needs to feel the love.* It's all
a slur, the room slides from under
and she's out the door, retching
from the back of a taxi, while
he holds her by the waist and rain
pounds the gutter clean.

Googling My Ex

I see you finally discovered your dwarf planet,
joined the community choir. Sorry I ruined your life,
though from what I can see you've recovered.
Nice leaf blower, and the Christmas lights!
What's it like to live in the same house for so long?
To know the insistence of a child for 31 years?
Let me tell you my spoonful—
that I've changed but not for the better.
Remember you and I, standing together,
Malibu beach on a blustery afternoon?
You're wearing those striped bell bottoms
and gaucho hat with a string tied under your chin.
I can only guess how I looked. The Pacific—
laid out before us, plain as clothes for Monday.

Crash (San Francisco, 1999)

Each time I try
to tell this story
I get it wrong.

No one understands
that when I describe
the way Mauro stepped

on top of the table, loaded
for dinner, I mean it
as a metaphor.

I mean, he really did it,
but when the table
collapsed under the weight

of a grown man who
should have known
better, it meant more

than eight guests frozen
in place for a few micro
seconds of splintering pine.

It was Christmas
but that's not
an essential detail.

More, is the way
it all slid—greasy
carcass, tiny salt dishes,

dessert plates smeared
with blueberries—as if
time slowed down.

More, is the way
you caught your cup—
and my eye—

with a flash of blue
just before it all
crashed to the floor.

We were astonished
at the bowl of mashed
yams that landed

right side up. I'll leave out
the part where Sharon
searched in vain

for her treasured
vodka shot glass.
What I mean to say is

that split second, when
Mauro's brain misfired,
foreshadowed all

that was to come,
including the exquisite
moment after

the last spoon settled,
when you pulled me close
and spun me

into a two-step,
and what I would give
to have that moment back.

Cleaning the Closet Suite

I.
I lost my toenails to the Jimmy Choos,
one size too small, apple-green,
out-of-season on sale. A bulky tunic
without a waistline is a wasteland.
That designer number hasn't aged well—
the lining bulges and drips
below the hem. A length
of metallic lace last worn
by Frida Kahlo, stuffed in a box.
Memory, that brittle petunia.

II.
My favorite capris have gone missing.
Black satin embroidered with butterflies,
lavender, peach, chartruese, sold
by every shop in Chinatown.
They drew delight and disdain
at the opera. I wore them
to the sheen of a bowling ball,
and to the dog-park mud that day
we celebrated another year
with Annie and the fog smelled
like iron and maybe a second chance.

III.
It was a sea-green dress.
I was wearing it when I met you.
I was wearing it when you left.
I wore it upside down

every Saturday night. It was
sleeveless and tight, hit me
just below the knees.
"Hurricane Hattie," Ralph
called it. I was at my best—
big hair full-bloom red. I wore it
the way I would the planet
Jupiter. I wore it for you.
And then I shrank it, folded
to a tiny square, tucked it
in your shirt pocket.
Slow-dancing, I can feel it
trembling even now.

Evidence

     It's a scene from The Outer Limits, the one where the
        townspeople disappear
              their coffee still warm
lidless jar of applesauce
     a few spoonfuls missing
         Yellow Pages next to the phone, opened to T for
                                 Incomprehensible

    His place is a map of sickness
or maybe a prayer
          empty bottles of Gatorade kneel on the coffee table
A detective in the forensics of loss, yet I can't trust my eyes
               blue jeans from every hook in the closet
                  molded to his shape
    his bed

I sniff for panic on his pillow, splay myself flat on the white flannel
                                   once *my* flannel
    what relief was he hoping to find between Towing and
    Transmission?

At the sink, the same braided rag rug where we stood together
                                   sun streaming
    behind me, pots soak their burned-out bottoms
        the turquoise ceramic plate brims with loose change
                          his keys are in my pocket

      Please don't let them come through the door just yet
to do what must be done for the dead

Two Figures in a Landscape
A painting by Willem de Kooning

That's you,
wearing an eye patch,
and there, that's me—
my delighted feet, pink
and fleshy. You're always here
at my shoulder when I look at art,
though today I can't remember
what you thought of de Kooning,
so I'm making it up.
After you died, I drove
an entire week with the plastic
canister of your ashes strapped
into the passenger seat and talked
to you, silence rising like blisters.
*For all the good it does, falling
on dead ears,* I could hear you say,
pleased with your joke. I wanted you
to paint the sun behind my eyelids.
Like this—crazy green,
a yellow cat stalking a bird,
wild with sky.

The Day the Widows Hijack the C Train

Widows are everywhere, you know—huddling
outside the ladies' room, rattling a jar for loose change,

binging on Jujubes, stoned at the movies. We line up
for the sauna with towels draped over our heads,

like a procession of novices, awkward in our habits.
Are we wringing or are we wailing?

We dig in designer bags for a tissue and come up
with a Ziplock of ashes to sprinkle in the Hudson.

Today, we're limping through Whole Foods in high heels
and black lace Miracle bras. We were up half the night,

giving alms to Tinder, and we're about to hijack
your morning commute—Myrtha and her ghost brides,
forever dancing men to their graves.

Four a.m.

For one thing, there are roosters.
The garbage-truck guy whistles
to signal the driver. I run into
Frank and Claire Underwood on
Pennsylvania Avenue, miner's lights
strapped to their heads. They look
the other way when I hop
on the American Flyer some kid
left out on the lawn, back wheel
still spinning. Claire mentions
her allergy to eggplant and how much
she misses veal at the White House.
I ask when Joan Jett will arrive.
She says, *Don't you think
it's a little early for so much black.*

Crossing Pleasure Avenue

In Sea Isle City, signs are posted:
Take it slow for the turtles.
Every summer they cross
the pavement from bay to beach.
Like us. Even if we don't give a whit
about turtles, we are compelled
to check our speed.

If we travel long enough
from the casino bus, Pleasure Avenue
will lead us to oldies night at Busch's,
where we can, if we're quick,
beat out the white haired ladies
for a place at the end of the bar,
to sit with our handbags swaddled
to our chests like the babies
we never had.

It's the best spot to sip a martini
and survey the kingdom of nothing
better to do on a Saturday night.
The dj spins tunes for women
with thickening midriffs, reclaiming
their youth on the dance floor.
We take our pleasure as we can.
When I pause just a beat too long
before saying no to the married guy
in the ballcap, the only guy
I want to dance with, who
do I think is watching?

Why do turtles lay their eggs
in the sand? God has his head
in the clouds. He flips a coin
to decide which side is the wrong
side. Watch as He sets a quarter
on the back of His thumb. Watch
the female turtles and their newborn
young take their marks along
Pleasure Avenue, the ocean side,
as the hot pavement sweats,
and once again risk everything.

On Leaving

For a week I've watched the osprey, roosting
with her brood. I know her flight path, landing loop,
the way she slides in, feet first. I've heard the demands
of her young, and yes, they are relentless.

It's Saturday—changeover day for the summer people.
I'm lingering on the deck when Mama Osprey
takes to the air yet again, this time heading
straight for me. Swooping low, she hovers

so close I can see her underbelly, feet dangling,
her presence hanging over me like judgment.
How could she know that I was a mother too?
That unlike her, I had a choice.

ACKNOWLEDGEMENTS

Thank you to the editors who first published these poems, some of which appeared in slightly different versions:

"Binomial Nomenclature" *It's Animal but Merciful*, great weather for MEDIA
"A History of Feminism" *The Other Side of Violet*, great weather for MEDIA
"When We Lived on Pineview Lane" *Southern Humanities Review*
"Dear John" *EDGE*
"We Need to Talk" *14 Hills*
"The Great Milky Way" *Maintenant 10*, Three Rooms Press
"Tough Bird" *Blue Mesa Review*
"All-American Activities" *Apalachee Review*
"Softball Game at the Church Picnic" *Whiskey Island*
"Sum Total" *Before Passing*, great weather for MEDIA
"Three Hour Train Delay" *Meridian Anthology*
"Home, ca 1951" *Glassworks*
"Good Fortune" *Blue Earth Review*
"Talking About the Heat" *West View* newspaper
"Learning to Paddle a Canoe" *Lindenwood Review*
"Dia de los Muertos" *Glassworks*
"Year of the Monkey" *Boog City Reader*
"Women Like Us" *A Gathering of the Tribes*
"A Woman in the Sun" *Slipstream*
"The Year of No Men" *The Year of Yellow Butterflies*, a blog by Joanna Fuhrman
"After the Wine Tasting" *The Journal*
"Femme Fatale" *Nimrod*
"Test Drive With Einstein" *Maintenant 8*, Three Rooms Press

"Winter" *Women Arts Quarterly*
"B Movie Fashion on the Red Carpet" *Boog City Reader*
"This is the Revolution" *Poetry Fix*
"Drought" *decomP magazine*
"Flood" *Stickman Review*
"Ode to My Bunion" *Boog City Reader*
"At Farley's" *Crack the Spine*
"Cleaning the Closet Suite" *Hiram Review*
"Evidence" *River Oak Review*
"Two Figures in a Landscape" *Poet Lore*
"The Day the Widows Hijack the C Train" *Boog City Reader*
"Crossing Pleasure Avenue" *gape seed*, Uphook Press

"A History of Feminism" was a finalist for the 2017 Disquiet Literary Prize.

These poems were adapted for the play, *The Old In and Out*, produced by Three Rooms Press (2013): "When We Lived on Pineview Lane"; "Sleep Apnea"; "The Haven"; "Earthquake Weather"; "Evidence"; "Crossing Pleasure Avenue."

"When We Lived on Pineview Lane" first appeared in a chapbook, *One Foot Out the Door*, published by Three Rooms Press (2005).

THANK YOU TO
the many poets, teachers and friends of my various writing communities who have given valuable feedback, support, and opportunity—most especially Kat Georges and Peter Carlaftes of Three Rooms Press, Joanna Fuhrman, Leanne Averbach and Jane Underwood, the first reader and writing partner whose absence I feel nearly every day.

Susan Parker, who inspired the title poem.

Julie Bruck for her encouraging and incisive manuscript review.

Alison Moore and Mark Rucker of Ravens' View Farm for hosting me as their first artist in residence.

Julio Cesar Martinez for the San Francisco skyline view from my beloved Potrero Hill that appears on the cover.

Michael Broder and Nicholas Oliver Moore of Indolent Books for their faith in this work.

 A third generation Colorado native, KAREN HILDEBRAND picked up at midlife and started over in San Francisco, then New York City. Her poetry has been published in many journals, nominated for Pushcart prizes and adapted for a play, "The Old In and Out," produced in NYC (2013). She is editor in chief of *Dance Teacher* magazine and chief content officer for DanceMedia Publications. She lives in Brooklyn.

INDOLENT BOOKS Indolent Books is a small nonprofit poetry press founded in 2015 and operating in Brooklyn, N.Y. Indolent publishes poetry by underrepresented voices whose work is innovative, provocative, and risky, and that uses all the resources of poetry to address urgent racial, social, and economic justice issues and themes.

Web: indolentbooks.com
Instagram: @indolent_books
Twitter: @IndolentBooks.